CONTENTS

KV-064-856

INTRODUCTION

People play sports for fun, to win, to break records and sometimes just to keep fit. The many different varieties of sport include ball games, athletic sports, water sports, winter sports, combat and target sports, to name just a few. Some sports are mechanical because they depend on, for example, racing cars or sailing boats. Others are played just for fun, for example bar-flying.

Some sports developed gradually over thousands of years. Archery, for example, started as a hunting skill. There are pictures of archers in 10,000-year-old Mesolithic cave paintings in Spain. Other sports date from recent times, like basketball, which was invented in 1891 in Springfield, Massachusetts, in the USA.

Sports science involves using scientific ideas to improve and develop sport. Science can help athletes to train effectively and can contribute to the design of new sports equipment. New records and new feats of endurance in sport occur all the time. Many are the direct results of scientific knowledge that is being applied to nearly every sport.

These people are bar-flying. Dressed in a Velcro suit, you jump from a small trampoline onto a Velcro-covered wall. You stick on the wall wherever you land!

Television and sport

There is nothing quite like being in the crowd at a big match. You experience the noise, the excitement – but if the goal is scored at the other end of the pitch, you just do not see it clearly! Sports photographers and TV cameras take pictures that capture such sporting moments. Yet how do the cameras get close enough to let everyone see exactly what happened when that goal was scored? This book will tell you.

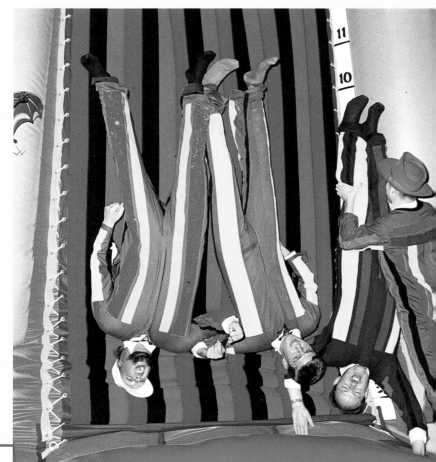

Today, sport is big business. The latest, 'high-tech' equipment allows athletes to shave hundredths of seconds off their times. Satellite television gives most people in the world the chance to watch major sporting events. People's interest in sport has never been greater, and the skill and abilities of athletes have never been higher. This book looks at the science behind some of the achievements athletes have made in sport.

Sport science in action

As our scientific knowledge increases, the manufacturers of sports equipment are continuously updating their designs and the materials they use. Between 1910 and 1980, the world pole vault record increased from 3.9 metres to 5.6 metres. Every ten years, on average, it regularly increased by about 20 centimetres. However, between 1960 and 1970, the record shot up by half a metre to 5.3 metres. What happened? Did pole vaulters train differently, or discover a wonder diet? No, they started to use a vaulting pole made of glass fibre. Athletes had experimented with aluminium and even bamboo poles, but glass-fibre ones gave the best results. The current world record is over 6 metres. Vaulting poles are now made from **carbon fibre**, which is lightweight but springy and very strong. Now even more astonishing records may be achieved.

Here you can see just how bendy a vaulting pole is.

SPINNING BALLS

Every golfer has at some time sliced a ball and watched it spin off in the wrong direction. In baseball, a good ball leaves the pitcher's hand spinning backwards at 1600 rpm (revolutions per minute). (A car engine ticks over, when stationary, at about 800 rpm.) It covers the distance from the pitcher's mound to the home plate (just under 18.5 metres) in 0.4 seconds. The ball travels at 160 kilometres per hour (kph) (100 mph) and only has time to spin ten or eleven times. The spin is enough to make the ball rise, or 'hop', over 10 centimetres in the air. Why do spinning balls swerve in the air?

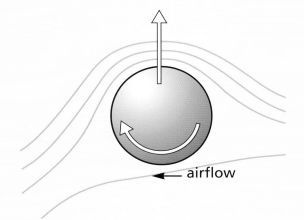

Magnus force

airflow

The pitcher can control just how the ball spins as it flies through the air. The diagram shows how the air flowing round the spinning ball causes it to change direction.

The spin factor

In baseball, the pitcher's grip controls the way that the ball spins. The pitcher can make the ball swerve, float or dip. (The speed record for the fastest ball, pitched by Nolan Ryan in 1974, is 162 kph or about 100 mph.) As air passes over the top of a ball that is spinning backwards, **friction** pulls some air part of the way around the back of the ball. This makes the trail left behind the ball in the air point downwards. Because air passing over the ball has further to travel, it moves faster. This produces an area of low pressure above the ball. The higher pressure under the ball lifts it! This is called the Magnus effect, after the German Heinrich Gustav Magnus (1802–70), who was Professor of Chemistry at Berlin University. It was he who described how a spinning ball experiences a sideways force.

Count the dimples

Someone discovered, by accident, that a damaged golf ball flies through the air better than a perfectly smooth one. So now all golf balls have dimples – the record number is 552. The shape and size of the dimples are important because they change the air flow around a ball in flight. Professional golfers want the balls they hit to have lots of spin because this helps to control the ball's direction accurately.

Today, more than one billion golf balls are made each year. Each one is made to an exact weight (not more than 50 grams) and diameter (not less than 4.27 centimetres). Golf balls that are designed to travel further have been banned in competitions – the golf courses would be too small!

A HAT FULL OF FEATHERS

The first golf balls were made of wood. They were replaced by balls made from a 'top-hat full' of boiled feathers. The feathers were stitched into three pieces of leather. As the ball dried, the feathers expanded and the leather shrank. Craftspeople could only make four balls a day, and for 250 years this is how golf balls were made!

RACKETS AND STRINGS

W hat do tennis rackets and aeroplanes have in common? They are both made from the same materials, which were developed for the aerospace industry. The first rackets with strings date from the fifteenth century and were made of wood. The frames were pear-shaped and not very strong, so their coarse gut strings were only loosely strung. Modern tennis rackets, like the rackets now used in sports such as badminton and squash, are made by combining different materials. Each material has its own special properties. What makes the rackets so strong and light?

Strong nylon strings

Plastics such as nylon are called **polymers**. They are made up of long **molecules**. Each molecule is made from smaller, identical molecules joined end to end. Rope is made strong by winding together long strands of fibres. In the same way, a polymer is strong because it consists of long lengths of joined-up molecules.

At the turn of the century, even Wimbledon champions played with wooden-framed tennis rackets.

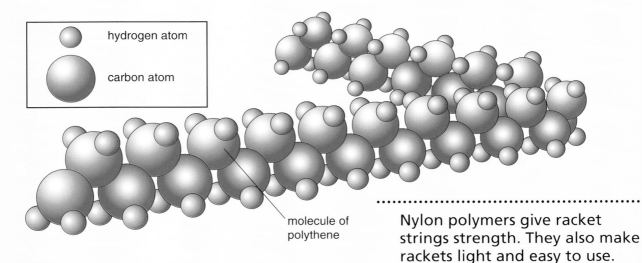

hydrogen atom

carbon atom

molecule of polythene

Nylon polymers give racket strings strength. They also make rackets light and easy to use.

Strong rackets

Metal tennis rackets were tried out in the 1920s, but then better wooden tennis rackets were developed. Their strong, light frames were made from thin strips of wood glued together. Professional players used these laminated rackets until the 1970s. The process of lamination 'lines up' the natural cellulose fibres of the wood, making the frame light and rigid. The same principle is used to make plywood.

The latest tennis racket frames are moulded using a combination of strong, light materials such as **fibreglass**, graphite and ceramics. Badminton, squash and racket ball rackets are also constructed from these materials, which are known as composites. In fibreglass, for example, thin glass fibres are embedded in plastic resin to form a remarkably tough material. A tennis racket frame made only from fibres of glass would not last long!

WHAT'S IN A NAME?

The name 'tennis' comes from the game that was originally played in France. The server called 'tenez', which means 'hold' in French, to warn the other players that the game was about to start.

Large-headed tennis rackets enable a player to control the ball better and also hit it faster than ever before.

Tough strings

Synthetic racket strings are made from as many as 48 separate plastic strands, called filaments. The strings are coated with silicone to protect them from wet and dirt. A tennis racket can be very tightly strung with these strings. Taut strings spring backwards and forwards more evenly, allowing the player to control the ball better. A player can hear if a racket is correctly strung by striking the strings and listening to the note!

Strings made of natural gut are still used in some rackets. They are more **elastic** than synthetic strings, and so they can be strung less tightly.

FASTER THAN THE WIND

Sailing craft can travel at very high speeds. A yacht at full speed sails at about 32 kph (20 mph), but the record for an ice yacht is more than 225 kph (140 mph). Sand yachts have reached speeds of nearly 145 kph (90 mph), and sail boarders regularly achieve speeds of more than 80 kph (50 mph). These speeds are much faster than the speed of the wind that fills the sails. How is this possible?

Across the wind

The sail of a yacht is not just a bag to catch the wind – it is like the wing of an aeroplane stood on end. When air passes over an aeroplane wing it reduces the pressure of the air above it. The higher pressure below 'lifts' the aircraft. Wind produces a similar difference in pressure across the curved sail of a yacht and, as a result, produces the force that drives the yacht forwards. The blades of an ice yacht prevent it from drifting sideways, so all the wind's energy goes into pushing the yacht forwards.

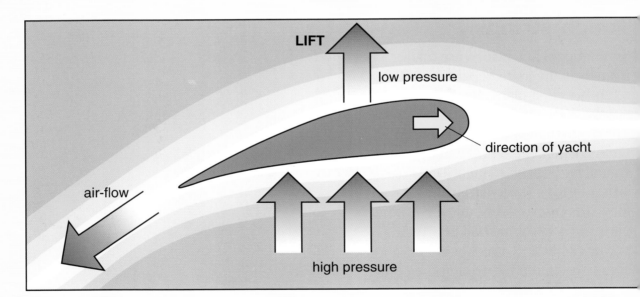

The curved, wind-filled sail of a yacht sailing at speed has much the same shape as the wing of an aircraft.

Reducing friction

Friction exists between any two surfaces that slide over one another. You can experience the force of friction by pushing your hand through water. A yacht has to overcome the force of friction between its hull and the water. The smooth sleek shape of the yacht's hull is designed to reduce friction. Ice yachts travel very fast because there is very little friction between their blades and the ice.

Friction affects the performance of a sand yacht too. Have you ever tried to ride a rusty old bicycle? You cannot turn the pedals because friction prevents the wheels from moving round. When you oil the wheels they turn smoothly. Oil reduces friction because it helps rough surfaces to slide over one another more easily. The wheels of a sand yacht have to be well lubricated.

SLIPPERY SHOES

Without friction, you would not be able to walk. Your shoes would slip on the pavement. When it is icy under foot, friction is reduced. This is why it is so easy to slip on an icy surface.

WINDY WEATHER

Winds are caused by the Sun's heat and the rotation of the Earth. You can understand the amount of energy in wind when you see the massive damage caused by a tornado or a great storm. This wind energy is used, or harnessed, by the sails of a yacht. It also helps the giant propellers on 'wind farms' to generate electricity.

Sand yachts can reach speeds of up to 145 kph (90 mph).

PEDAL POWER

Racing bicycles are built for speed. They have a strong but lightweight tubular frame. The drop handlebars allow the rider to be in a good position in order to turn the pedals easily. The large back wheel is driven by a chain through 12 or more gears. What do the gears on a bicycle do?

Changing gear

Gears help the rider to pedal more easily on steep slopes and on the flat. The cycle chain runs around a group of **gear wheels**, called sprockets. These are fixed to the back wheel. The biggest gear wheel probably has 30 teeth, the middle one 23 teeth and the smallest one only 13 teeth. Look at the big sprocket gears that the pedals turn. The largest one has 46 teeth. Suppose the cycle chain is running around the gears with 46 teeth and 23 teeth. This means that when you turn the pedals round once, the back wheel of the bicycle turns round twice. You are moving!

AS YOU STOP

When you are pedalling along energetically, you and the bicycle are both moving. Your body and the bicycle both have a certain amount of energy called **kinetic energy**. But what happens to that energy when you brake and stop? Energy cannot be created or destroyed; it can only be converted from one form to another. Friction between the brake pads and the wheel rims converts the kinetic energy into heat. Brakes are a convenient device for converting kinetic energy into heat! The rider's energy is also converted into heat.

A 'high-tech' time-trial bicycle. When gripping its forward-pointing handlebar, the helmeted rider is in the most streamlined position. Bikes like this one are designed to race on indoor tracks.

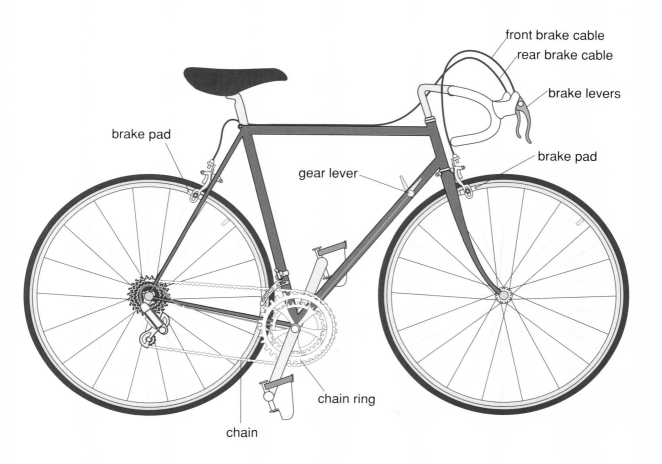

front brake cable

rear brake cable

brake levers

brake pad

gear lever

brake pad

chain ring

chain

When you change down into a lower gear, you turn the gripshift. It is notched so that it clicks into the right place for the next gear. A lower gear means that you need to use much less effort. It is ideal for going uphill because it gives you greater **mechanical advantage**.

Cables in control

When you twist the gripshift to change gear, or pull on the brake lever, you are using a lever to operate a cable control. The cable consists of a tough, steel wire which is threaded through a flexible metal tube. An outer plastic tube protects the metal one.

The brake lever is a simple lever that transmits (passes on) force in one direction only. The force is taken by cable to exactly where it is needed – where the brake pads press against the wheel.

SPEED ON SNOW

A speed skier races down a mountainside at more than 200 kph (125 mph) – the record to beat is now 238 kph (149 mph). This is higher than the speed of a **free-fall** parachutist – before the parachute opens! Only 30 years ago, 100 kph was fast for a downhill racer. So how do today's skiers go so fast?

Skis, bindings and boots

Modern skis are specially designed for different purposes. Speed skis, which are designed to travel fast in straight lines, have to be long and stiff. The shorter and narrower **slalom** skis need to turn easily. Skis are made by combining layers of different materials placed in a mould. The layers are glued together with an **epoxy resin**. Glass fibre is used to give strength and stiffness, and **Kevlar** fibres add strength.

As a skier starts a run, adrenaline, the hormone that speeds up **reaction times**, rushes into the bloodstream and the skier's heart rate reaches 200 beats per minute (the resting rate is about 70).

Smoother and faster

The underneath surface of a ski is made smooth with a coating of wax. The wax is applied while hot and it binds to the **polythene** outer layer of the skis. It can help a skier to take a second or two off a downhill course. Protective headgear is **streamlined** so that it offers little air resistance.

Speedy suits

A fast car is streamlined so it can pass through air with little disturbance to the flow of air around it. Any disturbance of the air, or **turbulence**, slows the car down. This is why ski suits are made from very smooth materials, just like the surface of a fast car or the hull of a yacht. They are designed to let the wearer slip through the air easily at high speed.

Foam-lined plastic boots with inflatable pads fit precisely around the skier's foot and ankle. They protect the skier from injury and help to control the skis.

Aluminium or plastic bindings attach the ski boots to the skis. They are adjusted to take into account the skier's weight, age, ability and size of foot. To prevent injury, they release automatically when a skier falls.

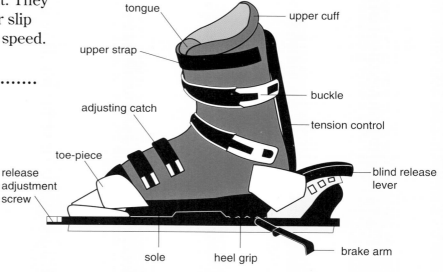

tongue

upper cuff

upper strap

adjusting catch

buckle

tension control

toe-piece

release adjustment screw

blind release lever

sole   heel grip

brake arm

SLED RACES AND MICROCHIPS

Sleds also go fast on snow and not just downhill! Each year in March, about 70 teams of fourteen or more huskies pull aluminium and ash sleds in a 1678-kilometre (1050 miles) race from Anchorage to Nome on Alaska's Bering Strait. This race, called the Iditerod, is the biggest sporting event in Alaska. To prevent teams from changing their dogs during the race, each animal is tagged with a **microchip** placed under the skin. The race takes eleven days.

SPECIAL SURFACES

Tennis courts, running tracks, soccer pitches and other kinds of sporting surface are made from a variety of different materials. Each type of surfacing material has advantages and disadvantages. For example, in sports such as soccer and tennis most of the action takes place on one part of the pitch or court. The centre of the soccer pitch and the penalty area wear out first, especially on a grass pitch. Most American football pitches are now plastic instead of grass, and not all of them are green! What other sports benefit from artificial surfaces?

Rain or shine

Older running tracks are made of grass, cinders or tarmac. These surfaces wear away because the lanes are used unevenly. Grass tracks become slippery when wet, but they can be used with most types of running shoe. Tarmac drains and dries easily, but athletes have to wear soft shoes on tarmac surfaces. Cinders are a traditional material and last for a long time, but they easily become waterlogged. Modern tracks are surfaced with tough synthetic rubber and **polyurethane** materials. They can be used for training and racing in all kinds of weather. They are designed to combine all the best features of the other types of surface.

This sports hall in Spain was built especially for the Olympic Games in 1992. Now games can be played in all weather.

Plastic snow

Many skiers practise on artificial ski slopes, especially during the warmer weather when there is no snow. The slopes are generally made of tufted nylon (like brushes). They provide enough friction for beginners to learn to ski and for advanced skiers to practise their skills all year round. Without friction, the skiers would slide down the slopes out of control.

Grass or clay?

Hard clay tennis courts allow the ball to bounce high and in a predictable way. This makes the game slower and easier for the players to control. On grass, the ball does not bounce as high, and is less predictable. So the game is very fast, and the outcome less certain!

SILENT RUNNING!

Several accidents took place on the running track during the 1976 Montreal Olympics. Some happened during distance events, and were blamed on the fact that the artificial track was 'silent'. Runners simply could not hear others running close behind!

Climbers, too, can train all year round. Walls constructed from polyester panels bolted to steel frames can be attached to the walls of halls or are used as free-standing structures. Climbing centres in major cities now have 15 metre walls, some of which are articulated (hinged) — the amount of overhang can be altered at will!

BEST FOOT FORWARD

Sports shoes have come a long way from the first canvas shoes with rubber soles. Now you can buy shoes designed especially for all major sports: athletics, football, tennis, basketball, baseball, and so on. Millions of pairs of sports shoes are sold all around the world. How can wearing a special shoe help you to perform better?

Inflatable shoes

Several shoe manufacturers, in particular Reebok, have designed inflatable sports shoes. A small air pump under the tongue of the shoe inflates a balloon-like bladder that surrounds the wearer's foot. This simple idea makes it possible to alter the shoe design to suit different sports.

Inflatable shoes provide a perfect fit for athletes. They can also provide the right kind of support. Tennis players' feet, for example, need very different support around the ankle and under the foot compared to, say, long-distance runners. This can be achieved very precisely by designing different shapes of inflatable bladder airbags to fit inside the various types of sports shoe.

In 1990, basketball players suddenly found they could jump higher when wearing the new Nike Air Jordan shoes. What made this shoe so special? It was inflatable.

A springy step

The feet of a running athlete pound the ground. Running shoes cushion the feet against these shocks by absorbing energy. Inside the midsole are built-in plastic tubes filled with air. As the midsole is squashed, the air inside these tubes is compressed. This stores energy which 'returns' to the athlete as the foot leaves the ground. As the plastic tubes spring back into shape, they push the athlete forwards. This results in the athlete's improved and faster performance.

Springy air!

When you pump up a bicycle tyre, the air inside the pump is being **compressed**. You can feel just how 'springy' this air is. This 'springiness' is called elasticity. It is the way in which some materials return to their original shape after they have been squashed or stretched. Rubber (and some plastics) are very elastic. This elastic quality of compressed air, together with the rubber-like materials used to make modern sports shoes, combine to make them better than ever before.

ADIDAS

In 1920 Adolf (Adi) and Rudolf Dassler began making the first specialist sports shoes in a small town near Nuremberg, Germany. The brothers invented running spikes, studs for football boots and screw-on crampons for mountaineers. The brothers gave their name to the multinational sports manufacturer Adidas.

(a)

(b)

The collar bladder (a) holds the heel in the rear of the shoe, and prevents it lifting out. This is good for activities like tennis or aerobics.
The arch bladder (b) gives support to the instep or 'arch' of the foot – important for long-distance runners.

SAFETY FIRST

In ice hockey, the fastest team game, players wear gloves, elbow pads, helmets, chest and shoulder padding and leg pads. Body armour like this is designed to absorb energy. Players of contact sports such as American football, as well as baseball players, also wear protective clothing. So what happens when something moving very fast is suddenly stopped?

Collision!

In snooker, you can see exactly how the momentum is transferred when two balls collide. When a moving ball strikes a stationary one squarely, the moving ball stops dead in its tracks and the other one shoots forwards. When you receive a blow to the side of the head, your brain moves, just like the stationary snooker ball. Your brain can be severely damaged as it collides with the inside of your skull.

What is momentum?

An object that is travelling along has **momentum**. Its momentum is calculated by multiplying the weight of the moving object by the speed at which it is travelling. So a small, light object that is travelling very fast can have the same momentum as a heavy, slow-moving object. In a collision, the momentum of the moving object is transferred to whatever it strikes.

The first American football helmets were made from boiled leather. Today's tough plastic helmets are fitted with unbreakable rubber-coated plastic face masks.

In ice hockey, the fastest team game, the players need gloves, elbow pads, helmets, chest and shoulder padding, and padding to protect their legs.

Buckle up!

So many American football players were killed or injured in the early 1900s that rules about protective clothing were changed.

Unlike a snooker ball, protective padding absorbs the energy transferred to it, and then spreads it out. Inside the helmets worn in American football are small containers or cells, filled with air or anti-freeze liquid. These prevent injury by spreading the effect of any impact evenly and by slowing it down. Players wear gum shields to protect their teeth. In addition to massive shoulder pads – some weigh 2.5 kilograms – rib pads with a hard plastic shell protect lower parts of the body.

SCARY SPEEDS

The tough plastic helmet worn by baseball players has to withstand the impact of a baseball travelling at 145 kph (90 mph). In ice hockey, the goal keeper's 'armour' has to protect them from a rubber puck travelling at 190 kph (118 mph)!

WHAT'S THE DAMAGE?

Many sports injuries are minor, like the muscle cramp sprinters get after a race. They do not cause any long-term damage to the athlete. Simple precautions, like warming up properly, help to avoid 'pulled' muscles. Muscles work better when they are 1° or 2°C above normal body temperature (around 37°C). Accidental injuries to muscles and bones have become accepted as a result of playing sport. So what are some of the more common sports injuries?

Joint damage

The ends of your knee bones, like the bones of other joints, are made of **cartilage**. It is softer than the rest of the bone (which it protects from damage). Skaters, runners, jumpers or footballers sometimes tear the cartilage in their knee. As a result, the knee joint swells up, is painful or even locks in position. An operation to remove the damaged cartilage may cure the problem.

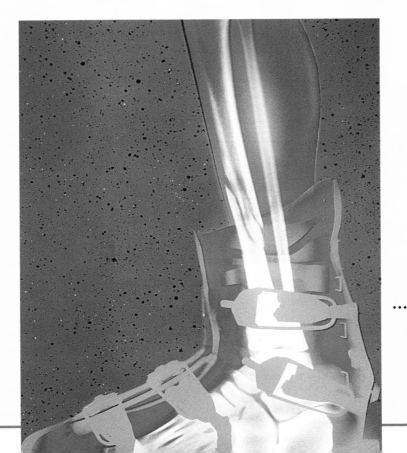

SWEATY WORK!

When you sweat your body cools down. This is because your body uses up 2260 joules of energy in order to evaporate 1 gram of water. Scientists use joules to measure energy. (An ordinary light bulb uses 100 joules of energy every second.) So it is the loss of energy that cools you! But as you sweat you lose salt, which is why sweat tastes salty! You need to replace this lost salt to keep the same concentration of salt in your body fluids, otherwise muscle cramp and even collapse can follow. An **isotonic** drink can help because it has the same overall concentration of salt as your body.

An X-ray reveals the tell-tale signs of another sports injury. Here, a skier's lower leg has been broken in a serious fall.

Knee and elbow joints work like hinges, or simple levers. Shoulder joints (and hip joints) are examples of ball and socket joints. The ball-like end of the arm bone, called the humerus, fits into a socket-like hole in the shoulder blade, or scapula. These joints can sometimes dislocate. When a rugby player falls awkwardly after a tackle, a shoulder may dislocate because the 'ball' literally comes out of the 'socket'. A physiotherapist can usually put the dislocated shoulder back in position.

Muscle wear and tear

A sharp blow to a muscle may burst a blood vessel. When this happens, blood collects in the muscle and clots. This causes a bruise which makes movement painful. 'Pulled' muscles are usually damage to a **tendon**. If you have a torn Achilles tendon (which attaches the calf muscle to your heelbone), you will probably have to walk with crutches for several months while the damage heals.

Despite heavy protective clothing, American footballers are likely to suffer from injuries at some point in their career.

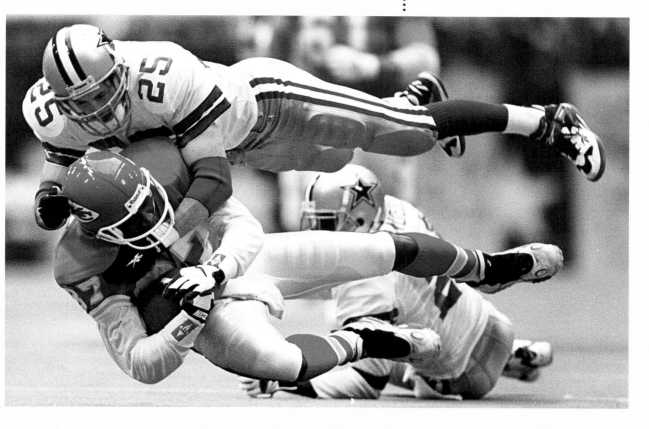

WORKING OUT

Your heart beats about 70 times a minute. That is nearly 37 million times each year! Your heart is made of a special kind of muscle – it performs without tiring. A healthy person is unaware of these muscles working and (usually) of those involved in breathing. The muscles you use to move your arms and legs are called skeletal muscles; like your heart muscles, they need energy to work properly. Working out helps you to use the energy you get from your food effectively. How do your muscles, breathing and blood circulation work together?

Are you fit?

The Harvard step test is one way to find out how fit you are. You step up and down every 2 seconds for 5 minutes. The step should be half a metre high. After resting for a minute, you take your pulse by counting your heart beat for 30 seconds. After a 30-second pause, you check your pulse again and, after another 30-second pause, once more. If you are fit, your heart rate should slow down and recover quickly after taking exercise. If your heart rate takes a long time to slow down, then you are not as fit as you could be. The normal pulse rate of an athlete may be only 30 beats a minute because the athlete's blood circulation has improved as a result of fitness training. Tiny blood vessels can enlarge by as much as five times during exercise. Blood circulation is boosted at the start of a race when a **hormone** called adrenaline speeds up an athlete's heartbeat. It rushes into the bloodstream, making the athlete's heart rate reach around 200 beats a minute.

'Step' exercises are great fun. They are also a superb way to increase fitness and develop a healthy heart.

A breath of air

How does the oxygen in the air reach your blood?
You have tiny air sacs called alveoli in your lungs.
They are surrounded by tiny blood vessels. Here
oxygen passes from your lungs into your blood.
The fitter you are, the more efficiently your lungs
work and the more oxygen they take from the air
each time you breathe.

Training for your sport

To be fit you need to have stamina, flexibility, speed
and strength. Each sport demands a different
training programme that concentrates on a
particular aspect of fitness. A swimmer, for
example, must have stamina; sprinters need speed;
a weightlifter is, above all, strong, and gymnasts
need to be flexible.

The passage of oxygen into the blood. Air
sacs called alveoli collect air from the lungs
and send out oxygen to the blood vessels
around them.

BURNING IT UP

Do you know how much
energy is in the many
foods you eat? You can
find out by looking at
the labels on packaged
foods, which give the
amount of energy per
100 grams of food. A
Mars bar has 990
kilojoules (1 kilojoule, or
kJ, equals 1000 joules)
and an egg 310 kJ. The
energy you get from
eating food is released
in your muscles
whenever you move. A
footballer playing for
1 hour, for example,
might 'burn up' 2260 kJ.

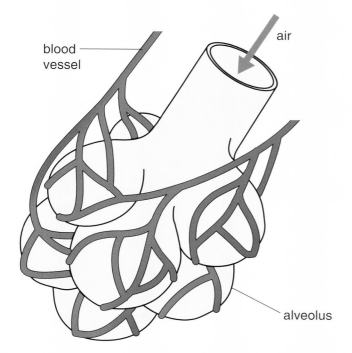

blood vessel

air

alveolus

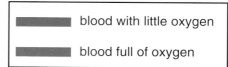

blood with little oxygen

blood full of oxygen

KEEPING THE SCORE

Think about two sporting events with different ways of scoring. In a figure skating competition, the result for one skater may be 7.8. This is an average of all the scores from the judges. Each judge decides separately how well the skater performed, and some award a higher score than others. The score in a football match is different; a result of 3–2 clearly means that the team which scored 3 goals has won. The results in many other sports, such as sprinting and javelin throwing, depend on precise measurement. How do we make sure that these measurements are accurate?

It's a record

In most school and amateur athletics competitions, the timekeepers use stopwatches. They wait by the finishing line, finger on the button. When the starter's pistol fires, they press the buttons to start the stopwatch. They wait by the finishing line and as the winner crosses the tape they stop the watch. Now it takes about 10 seconds to run 100 metres. The times of the different timekeepers are averaged. Clearly an error of 0.1 seconds makes a huge difference when there may only be a difference of 0.01 seconds separating first and second place. Now compare this to a 10,000-metre race (which takes about 30 minutes). The same error of 0.1 seconds is much less important. At major sporting events, the timing is now entirely electronic. The electronic clock starts automatically as the starting pistol fires. By linking the clock to the starting blocks, false starts can also be detected!

Electronic scoreboards and giant video screens are just two of the developments that have revolutionized the way we watch and enjoy sport.

Quick as a flash!

Everyone has a **reaction time**. This is the time it takes, for example, for an athlete to hear a starting pistol and start running. The reaction time is generally not much more than 0.1 seconds! A Grand Prix driver might have a reaction time of about 0.2 seconds. The reaction time of a timekeeper operating a stopwatch, or of a linecourt judge in a tennis match, may well change the result of a race or a match!

Was that serve in?

Electronic equipment is also used in a sport like tennis to decide whether the ball is good. As it leaves the server's racket, the ball can travel at over 190 kph (120 mph). At this speed, there is often a difference of opinion between the player and the line-court judge. An electronic eye can 'see' exactly where the ball lands. It shines three beams of infra-red light behind the service box line or the back line of the court. When all three beams of light are blocked out by the ball, the electronic eye beeps loudly to signal that the ball is out.

'ON YOUR MARKS'

When starting pistols were first used in athletics competitions, timekeepers started their watches when they heard the bang. But sound takes 0.3 seconds to travel 100 metres! Now timekeepers start their watches when they see the smoke from the pistol, because light travels at 300,000,000 metres per second.

The race is over, but the work has just begun for the judges who have to decide the final winner.

MILLIONS WATCHED

Watching sport has always been popular, but now television allows many people to watch one event, as it happens. Television made it possible for 33.4 million people in the USA to watch the 1993 XXVII Superbowl. This was a record for a single programme. Now some major events can only be seen on satellite television, unless you are actually present in the audience! Television, together with telephoto camera lenses and slow-motion photography, have changed the way we see sport.

BILLIONS OF VIEWERS

In 1990, 26.5 billion TV viewers watched the football World Cup finals.

Close-up work

When you use a magnifying glass, you hold it a certain distance from the object to focus the image sharply. A camera lens focuses in the same way. The distance for an ordinary 35-millimetre camera lens is about 50 millimetres. This is called the focal length. A telephoto lens can focus at four times the same distance (200 millimetres); it enlarges the image 16 times. Such lenses are like short telescopes because everything you see through them looks much closer than it really is.

A zoom lens is a telephoto lens with a focal length that can be changed to make the image fill the frame. Skilled camera operators can use these lenses to follow a race leader or a goal scorer.

Slow motion

A disputed goal, two horses finishing exactly together, a serve that is called out – these are things that happen often in sport. The TV viewer can often see the disputed moment again, in slow motion. How is this done? A normal movie film is made by taking 24 separate pictures every second. You do not see the pictures separately because your eyes carry on seeing something after it is no longer in front of them. This is called **persistence of vision**. Your eyes take time to adjust to each new picture. If you look at a film played at half-speed, then the action also slows down to half-speed. This is slow motion.

Pictures around the world

Communications satellites constantly orbit the Earth. They travel at just the right speed to stay over the same part of the globe. Radio and television signals, which can only travel in straight lines, are beamed up by a satellite dish in one country to the nearest communications satellite. It boosts the signal, using energy from its solar panels. The signal is then beamed back to a satellite dish in another country. In this way, a football match can be seen on television all round the world as it is being played.

Television companies are constantly finding new ways of getting you closer to the action. Cameras on rails can follow every move of a footballer as he runs up the pitch.

GLOSSARY

carbon fibre a very pure and fine fibre made of carbon. It is used to reinforce plastic materials to make them strong.

cartilage the soft tissue where bones meet together. The same kind of tissue also supports the ears, nose and larynx (voice-box).

compress squeeze something together so that it occupies a smaller space

elastic something that regains its normal shape by itself after being stretched or squashed

epoxy resin a plastic material that sets very hard. It is used to make electrical equipment and also adhesives.

fibreglass strong plastic material reinforced with matting made from finely spun glass fibres, sometimes called GRP or glass reinforced plastic

free-fall falling freely through the atmosphere, usually before the parachute opens

friction the force between two surfaces rubbing together which slows their movement and produces heat

gear wheel a wheel with teeth spaced regularly around its rim

isotonic drinks solutions of chemical substances adjusted not to disturb the chemical balance of substances in an athlete's body

Kevlar a synthetic material so strong that it can be woven into bullet-proof vests, or twisted into cables stronger than steel

kinetic energy the energy a moving body has because it is moving

mechanical advantage the amount by which your effort is multiplied, for example, by a car jack which enables you to lift the car up

microchip a complete electronic circuit built on a small piece of silicon, used in computers, cars, radios, televisions, etc.

molecule the smallest amount of a substance that exist by itself and still have all the same properties as the substance

momentum the impetus or tendency of any body in motion to go on moving

persistence of vision when the eye continues to see an object in the same place after it has moved a little

polymer a chemical substance made by joining together many repeating units of a simpler chemical substance. It can be natural, like cellulose in wood, or synthetic, like many plastics such as polythene.

polythene a plastic material or polymer made by joining together many repeating units of a simpler chemical substance, in this case ethane, a gas obtained from petroleum

polyurethane a plastic material used to make adhesives, paints, varnishes, plastics and rubbers, also used as a foam for insulation

reaction time the time it takes someone to react after they have seen something; for example to apply the brakes of a car after seeing a dog run across the road

slalom a ski race down a zig-zag course marked out by flag poles

streamline the shape of vehicle, for instance, which presents the least resistance to motion. The shape of a fish is a good example.

tendon the strand of very strong tissue that connects a muscle to bone

turbulence the irregular flow of air or fluid around an obstacle

FACTFILE

- In 1980 there were four left-handers in the top ten places in the world tennis rankings. At the world table-tennis championships, there were six left-handers in the top ten. Some people believe that left-handers have a quicker reflex than right-handers. This 'leftie advantage' seems to be useful in fencing, boxing, squash and cricket, as well as tennis. However, not all experts agree about it.

- Athletes increasingly think through in great detail what they are going to do when competing in important events. This is called visualization. Javelin throwers, for example, will 'see' exactly how they might make a perfect throw. When it comes to the real thing, their throw is likely to be better as a result! The modern javelin, which weighs only 800 grams, can be thrown over 100 metres. In fact, it is designed so that it is not perfectly aerodynamic – otherwise it might be thrown into the crowd or even out of the stadium.

- Modern chemical techniques are used to detect minute amounts of drugs in sportspeople. Some people take drugs to build up their muscles and increase their stamina. Athletes and other sportspeople are regularly tested. This can be done easily with a urine sample. It is accurately analysed in a laboratory. Very accurate instruments are used to identify any suspect substance in the urine.

- Many records would be smashed in an athletics meeting on the Moon. The Moon's gravity is six times weaker than the gravity on Earth, so there is less pulling force to keep you on the surface of the Moon. High-jumpers should do pretty well on the Moon! A shot-putter would make a throw literally out of this world!

INDEX